H 1015

CARL CZERNY

The School of Velocity

(Complete)

Op. 299

EDITED AND FINGERED WITH COMMENTARY
BY
GARY BUSCH

THE
F·J·H
MUSIC
COMPANY
INC.

Frank J. Hackinson

Production: Frank J. Hackinson
Production Coordinator: Satish Bhakta
Consulting Editor: Edwin McLean
Interior Design: Susan Pinkerton
Printer: Tempo Music Press, Inc.

THE
F·J·H
MUSIC
COMPANY
I N C.
Frank J. Hackinson

ISBN 1-56939-495-4

CARL CZERNY

The School of Velocity, Op. 299

Carl Czerny in 1839
Lithograph by S. Parmenter

H1015

TABLE OF CONTENTS

THE SCHOOL OF VELOCITY, OP. 299

ABOUT CARL CZERNY

Life

arl Czerny was born February 21, 1791, the only child of Wenzel Czerny, a Bohemian music teacher who had settled in Vienna five years earlier. Since many of his students were too poor to pay for music lessons, Wenzel Czerny's income as a piano teacher was modest. He frequently exchanged instruction of his pupils for tutoring services for Carl, which included lessons in Italian, French, German, and literature.

From an early age Carl exhibited the extraordinary diligence and self-motivation that would ensure his later success. Under his own initiative he began composing when he was only seven years old, and by the age of 10 was able to perform from memory nearly every piano work of Mozart and Clementi, among other major composers. He made his first public appearance with orchestra at the age of nine, performing Mozart's *Concerto in C Minor, K. 491.*

At a time during which Beethoven had yet to gain acceptance by the musical establishment, firsthand reports of the composer's work came to the Czerny family through a close mutual friend, violinist Wenzel Krumpholz. Krumpholz's introduction of the 10-year-old Carl Czerny to Beethoven marked the beginning of a long and important relationship. Carl later recalled their memorable first meeting on a wintry day, accompanied by his father and Krumpholz:

I had to play something right away, and since I was too bashful to start with one of his works, I played the great C Major concerto by Mozart [K. 503]. Beethoven soon took notice, moved close to my chair, and played the orchestral melody with his left hand whenever I had purely accompanying passages . . . . When he expressed satisfaction, I felt encouraged enough to play his recently published *Sonata Pathétique* and finally the *Adelaide,*

which my father sang with his very respectable tenor voice. When I had finished, Beethoven turned to my father and said, "The boy is talented, I myself want to teach him and I accept him as my pupil. Let him come several times a week. But most important get him [Carl Philipp] Emanuel Bach's book on the true art of clavier-playing,[1] which he must have by the time he comes to see me again.[2]

The roots of Carl's technical approach stem directly from his lessons with Beethoven, who stressed scales in all keys, and fundamentals that included proper positioning of the hands, fingers, and thumb. Beethoven also emphasized the new *legato* approach, yet unknown to other pianists steeped in the still fashionable detached *Hammerflügel* technique of Haydn and Mozart.[3] Beethoven's formidable improvisational skills were well documented by his contemporaries, and Czerny was fortunate to have had the elder master extemporize for him privately on a regular basis. These valuable skills would be passed on directly to Czerny's students and appeared in several of his published treatises on improvisation.

Beethoven's increasing involvement in composition and the inability of Carl's father to continue accompanying his young son to lessons led to a gradual cessation of the instruction. Carl did, however, continue to move within the most important Viennese musical circles. From 1801 to 1804 he and his father attended musical soirées hosted by Mozart's widow, where he met and heard Hummel[4] play.

In 1804, Carl was introduced by Krumpholz to one of the composer's most ardent patrons, Prince Lichnowsky, who had first brought Beethoven to Vienna. By this time Czerny had committed all of Beethoven's music to memory. The 13-year-old visited Prince Lichnowsky for several hours daily, during which he played from the repertoire of the composer's works on request. At the prince's house Czerny reestablished contact with Beethoven. He read from sight the newly composed *Waldstein Sonata* from the composer's manuscript. From then on, Czerny became a close confidante of Beethoven, proofreading his newest compositions, and producing piano reductions of his opera *Fidelio* and other large works.

In 1810 Czerny formed an influential association with the celebrated pianist, composer, pedagogue, publisher, and piano manufacturer Muzio Clementi when Clementi visited Vienna. As a friend of Clementi's host family, Czerny was able to spend time observing the master teacher's lessons with the daughter of the house, an experience that Czerny claimed as an important influence on his own teaching technique.

Czerny's performance of Beethoven's first piano concerto at the age of 15 marked the beginning of his public reputation as a noted interpreter of the composer's works. Despite his formidable abilities as a performer, however, Czerny opted at this time to abandon concert touring in favor of devoting his energies to teaching and composition. The many accomplished students that he soon produced allowed him to raise his lesson fees, putting an end to his family's longstanding financial instability. During this period he studied books on thoroughbass[5] and other music theory, and produced as many compositions as his increasing teaching load would permit.

Beginning in 1816 Czerny taught 11 or 12 lessons daily from 8 A.M. to 8 P.M., with evenings and any other bits of available time dedicated to composing. The same year he also began giving weekly all-Beethoven recitals, which were attended by many admirers, including the composer himself. During his active teaching years Czerny was sought as a teacher by the most prestigious families and developing musicians in Vienna and beyond. One of these, the young Franz Liszt, was brought by his father to Czerny one morning in 1819. Czerny recalled his first impressions of the eight-year-old prodigy:

He was a pale, delicate-looking child and while playing swayed on the chair as if drunk so that I often thought he would fall to the floor. Moreover, his playing was completely irregular, careless, and confused, and he had so little knowledge of correct fingering that he threw his fingers over the keyboard in an altogether arbitrary fashion. Nevertheless, I was amazed by the talent with which nature had equipped him. I gave him a few things to sight-read which he did, purely by instinct, but for that very reason in a manner that Nature herself had here created a pianist. He made the same impression when I acceded to his father's wish and gave him a theme on which to improvise. Without the least bit of acquired knowledge of harmony he yet managed to convey a feeling of inspiration in performance.[6]

As only a minor official of the Esterházy estate, Liszt's father was of insufficient means to provide lessons for his son from the greatest piano pedagogue of the day. Czerny generously offered to oversee young Franz's progress, which he did nearly every evening for two years. For his young student, he concentrated rigorously on building musical foundations that included scales in all keys, a strong feeling of rhythm, sensitive touch and tone, and correct fingering. He instilled in him the "spirit and character" of various composers through the works of Hummel, Ries, Moscheles, Clementi, Beethoven, and Bach.[7] He also required Liszt to learn these works rapidly, in an effort to develop his sight-reading to such a degree that he could perform difficult works in public as perfectly as if he had been studying them extensively. The diet of musical skills was completed with improvisation study, in which Liszt was called upon to elaborate on given themes.

Czerny continued his industrious regimen of teaching and composing until 1836, when the constant strain that overwork imposed on his health finally forced him to abandon teaching. His remaining years continued, however, to be filled with creating hundreds more compositions and pedagogical writings – and caring for his houseful of cats.[8] Upon his death in 1857, the characteristically generous Czerny left his estate to Viennese musical organizations and to various charities for the needy and handicapped.

Significance

Carl Czerny's varied musical output encompasses original and arranged compositions for solo and ensemble piano, chamber music, symphonies, and sacred choral works. It is, however, for his astounding number of pedagogical works that he is most celebrated. Czerny, along with Muzio Clementi and Johann Cramer have been referred to as the "Three C's" of piano pedagogy[9], much in the same way that Bach, Beethoven, and Brahms symbolize the indispensable triune core of the piano repertory. Czerny's influence as a teacher remains without parallel in the history of music. Besides nurturing many of the greatest pianists of the 19th century, he was the first to systematize in the greatest detail the technical system for the newly established pianoforte.

Among his nearly 1,000 works lie treatises on every imaginable aspect of music. The titles of several of these provide a glimpse of his astonishing versatility and mastery within the field: *Systematic Guide to Improvisation on the Piano, Opp. 200 and 300, School of Fugue Playing, Op. 400, Complete Theoretical and Practical Pianoforte School, Op. 500,* and *School of Practical Composition, Op. 600.* Of particular interest is the *Umriss der Ganzen Musik-Geschichte bis 1800, Op. 815* ("Outline of Music History since 1800 in its Entirety"), a tabular rendering of the gamut of music history up to his time.

As the pupil of Beethoven and teacher of Liszt, Carl Czerny constitutes the critical link between Beethoven and pianists of today. His detailed reports of Beethoven's playing are among the most valuable documents regarding Beethoven's performance style, and his editions of Scarlatti and J.S. Bach's *Well-Tempered Clavier* reflect the manner in which they were taught to him by the older master.

Czerny's influence continued past his lifetime through the two greatest pedagogues of the late 19th century. Franz Liszt brought piano technique to its next stage of evolution, and trained an entire generation of concert pianists during his semi-retirement in Weimar, Germany. The famed piano pedagogue Theodore Leschetizky, whose revered "Leschetizky method" became the foundation for many celebrated virtuosi whose careers extended into the early 20th century, was among these students. Of his much-acclaimed skill at producing countless great pianists like Ignaz Paderewski, Benno Moisiewitsch, and Artur Schnabel, Leschetizky would later assert, "I have no method. I teach piano as it was taught to me by my master Czerny."[10]

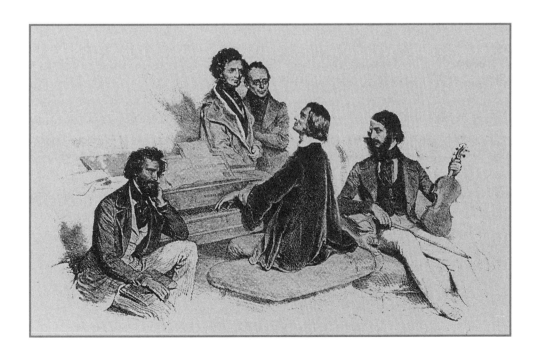

An Afternoon with Liszt
Lithograph by Kriehuber
l. to r.: Josef Kriehuber, Hector Berlioz, Carl Czerny, Franz Liszt (seated at the piano), Heinrich Ernst.

CZERNY'S STYLE AND TECHNIQUE

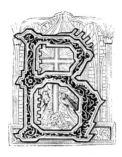 orn in the year of Mozart's death, Czerny witnessed the transition between the fading keyboard technique of the end of the 18th century and that required at the dawn of the emerging Romantic period. Mozart's technique had been inherited from the harpsichord, employing the fingers and hand exclusively, with a predominantly *staccato* touch.[11] Through Beethoven, Czerny acquired the *legato* touch that would soon represent the mainstay of Romantic style. His perceptive concepts also advocated the most natural physical manner in which to approach the newly popular instrument.

The continuing evolution of the piano over the generation following Czerny's produced a more powerful instrument with a heavier touch, and with it new technical challenges. Unfortunately, alongside this development emerged a technical school that advocated the immoderate employment of exercises with a stiff, immobile arm, highly raised fingers, and a percussive tone, a reactionary throwback to baroque and early classical harpsichord technique.[12] This approach exemplified by the Lebert-Stark method,[13] developed in the mid-19th century at the Stuttgart Conservatory and was perpetuated throughout Europe for several generations. Technical studies like those of Czerny have often unfairly become the undeserving recipients of criticism from future generations, who became aware of the potential for injury under thoughtless extremes and questionable technical practices. As with many beneficial tools, piano exercises are valuable when executed under competent supervision with sound principles, as clearly exemplified in Czerny's teaching and treatises. While an extended presentation of a topic as expansive as technique is beyond the scope of this commentary, a summary of Czerny's attitudes regarding general technical principles would be helpful in dispelling modern misconceptions regarding his methods.

On the use of exercises:

The astounding number of exercises that Czerny produced might mislead the modern world into assuming that such exercises constituted the core of his teaching. To the contrary, because of their potential for tediousness Czerny specifically cautioned that exercises not be inflicted on students in excess, but used supplementally and only in moderation. Emphasized instead was the importance of developing the pupil's taste through the selection of stimulating repertoire.[14]

On freedom of the arm:

Unlike Lebert-Stark, Czerny had, in the previous generation, promoted the modern concepts of an arm freed from the shoulder downward[15] and the modern concept of arm weight, in lieu of a locked arm from which the wrist or elbow would function as hinges:

Before anything else, it must be observed that the crescendo should never be produced by a visible exertion of the hands, or by lifting up the fingers higher than usual when we are playing legato; but only by an increased internal action of the nerves, and by a greater degree of weight, which the hand receives therefrom, without however fettering the flexibility of the fingers.[16]

On use of the fingers:

Czerny also did not advocate the percussive action of overly elevated fingers used by the later Stuttgart school, stating

> ...each finger, previous to its being used, must be held very near to its key (without however touching it), so after the stroke, it must again return to its previous situation .... The hand must ... be held as tranquilly as possible over the five keys, so that the reiterated percussion may be produced by the quiet movement of the single finger.

For very rapid passages Czerny described a special type of finger action, which he termed a *mezzo staccato* or "dropped notes" touch:

> ... each finger with its soft and fleshy tip on the keys makes movement like that used in *scratching* or in *tearing* off something, employs more or less of the rapid action of the nerves and muscles, and thereby obtains a very clear, pearly, and equal touch, by which, even in the quickest times, all passages may be executed with equal roundness and finish, with a full and not too harsh tone, and with the most perfect and pleasing tranquillity of the hands.[17]

On freedom of the body:

In a series of explanatory pedagogical letters written to an imaginary young lady, Czerny also promoted the elimination of unnecessary gestures, but warned equally against a rigid body stance:

> ... we may play with great power, without any excessive exertion, and without using any unnecessary and ridiculous movements of the hands, arms, shoulders, or head. For, unhappily, many even very good pianists are guilty of these and similar contortions and grimaces against which, . my dear girl, I must warn you .... Do not suppose, however, that you are to sit at the piano as stiff and cold as a wooden doll. Some graceful movements are *necessary* while playing; it is only the *excess* that must be avoided.[18]

On differentiating among styles and technical approaches:

Based largely on 18th-century arpeggio and scale technique, Czerny's pedagogical works constitute the crowning summation of technique in the early 19th century. Yet, the ever modest Czerny was aware that his generation could not reasonably claim to represent the summit of evolution of piano technique, but differentiated among six different schools of playing. These ranged from that of Mozart to a new style that was

> ... just now beginning to be developed, which may be called a mixture of an improvement on all those which preceded it. It is chiefly represented by Thalberg, Chopin, Liszt, and other young artists; and is distinguished by the invention of new passages and difficulties, and consequently the introduction of new effects – as also by an extremely improved application of all the mechanical means, which the piano-forte offers in its present greatly improved state, and which, like all former improvements in their day, will give a new impulse to the art of playing on this much cultivated instrument.[19]

Building on the superb foundation provided by their former teacher, Liszt, Leschetizky, and other Czerny students would find themselves at the helm of these future developments.

GUIDE TO
THE SCHOOL OF VELOCITY

entral to *The School of Velocity* lies the goal of building velocity employing the full range of dynamics and touches. Czerny's metronome markings are reproduced in this edition exactly as they appeared in the earliest published sources. It must be stressed, however, that these were intended for an instrument with a lighter action and different resonance characteristics than the pianos of today. The editor therefore advises modern users that many of these indications might be considered as being of historical interest, rather than necessarily as actual tempi to which to aspire. In any case, velocity will be achieved most quickly through sensible application of sound technical principles, such as proper hand position and relaxation, and not by pressing tempi unreasonably beyond the limits of one's current level of accomplishment.

A brief description of the technical features of each exercise will aid in a general survey of the collection and the selection of appropriate studies:

BOOK 1

1 C Major
Right-hand scales, descending and ascending, accompanied by simple sustained left-hand chords.

2 C Major
Ascending left-hand scales, followed by descending (mm. 15-19). Right-hand double note counter-melody with brief scalewise terminations.

3 C Major
Continuous ascending and descending broken arpeggios in successive inversions for both right and left hands.

4 C Major
Right-hand 1-2-3-4 study focusing on passing the thumb under 2, and 2 over the thumb. Simple on-beat left-hand chords throughout.

5 C Major
Extensive scale study for both hands, separately, and together in tenths. Left-hand ascending scale patterns set against a right hand of varying articulations, first in mixed *legato/staccatissimo* (mm. 15-23) and later in two-voice *legato* counterpoint (mm. 35-38).

6 C Major
Right-hand study for even execution of adjacent three-note groupings using 5-4-3, 4-3-2, and 3-2-1.

7 C Major
Leggiero left-hand study of repeated four-note accompanimental groupings, set against a two-voice right hand of mixed articulations.

8 C Major
Extensive right-hand study of narrow and extended scale passagework. Contracted hand positions alternating with expanded ones that include broken four-note arpeggios.

9 C Major
Extensive study of short and extended scale passagework with equal alternation between the hands. *Subito* changes of dynamics in velocity.

10 F Major
Constant left-hand Alberti bass against lyrical right hand with varied *legato/staccatissimo* articulations.

BOOK 2

11 C Major
Right-hand study in descending and ascending diatonic broken thirds set against a left-hand detached accompaniment.

12 F Major
Ascending and descending arpeggios in parallel motion, hands at the octave.

13 B♭ Major
Left hand dropping on-beat against right-hand three-note rotations in *toccata* style. Clearly modeled after J.S. Bach's B♭ Prelude from the *Well-Tempered Clavier, Bk. I*, making this an excellent supplement for the study of that work. Climax (mm. 49-56) features left-hand *legato* octaves accompanied by right-hand broken, descending, four-note chords.

14 F Major
Varying right-hand extensions of 5-1, followed by extended mordent figurations that involve passing 2 over the thumb.

15 C Major
Four-note patterns with 1-2-3-4, mostly for the right hand. Varying extensions between 4-1 and single-note passing between 4-1.

16 G Major
Right-hand stepwise broken thirds and sixths in compound meter.

17 F Major
Division of right-hand thirds into sustained and active accompanying elements, which are reversed in the second half. Left-hand broken stride accompaniment throughout.

18 G Major
Left-hand velocity study in descending and ascending broken, three-note, sequential groupings.

19 F Major
Thumb-pivot study of five-note broken arpeggios for the right hand. Left hand divided into sustained *legato* bass line and off-beat chords.

20 C Major
Rotation between all intervals from the second to the octave. Hands parallel at the tenth throughout.

BOOK 3

21 C Minor
Rapid right-hand accompaniment integrating four-note rising and falling scales with brief octave extensions. Sustained melody emerging within the right-hand pattern in the central episode (mm. 17-24). Left hand alternates between two-voice melodic counterpoint and block chord accompaniment.

22 G Major
4-3-2-1 repetition, left hand and right hand alone and together.

23 A Major
Extended compound-meter, right-hand rotation study with much variety.

24 D Major
Downward four-note scale and arpeggio groupings alternating with scales. Left-hand accompaniment of two-note slurs, two-voice counterpoint (mm. 7, 21-4), and double notes (mm. 27-49).

25 E♭ Major
Ascending and descending scale study with hands mostly parallel at the octave throughout.

26 A Major
Right-hand alternations between symmetrical and asymmetrical polyrhythmic scalewise groupings of 9, 10, 11, 12, and 13 against left-hand broken chords with sustained bass notes.

27 B♭ Major
Gently sustained *pianissimo* soprano/bass duet, set against delicate tremolos in the alto and tenor, dividing both hands into melodic and accompanimental elements.

28 C Major
Right-hand rotation of 4-5 alternating with thumb, against simple left-hand stride accompaniment.

29 F Major
Varied study employing scales, hands together at the third, sixth, and tenth, alternating with right-hand passages of four-note broken arpeggios and ascending/descending scales.

30 C Major
Primarily stepwise progressions of four-note arpeggios divided between the hands. Opening of second half features five-note arpeggios with wide crossings in the right hand. Brilliant *fortissimo* throughout.

BOOK 4

31 B♭ Major
Chromatic study emphasizing 1-2-3 for both hands separately and together.

32 C Major
Ascending and descending four-note legato arpeggios divided between the hands.

33 E Major
First half of study features three-note groupings of 3-2-1 and 4-3-2 and extended scales for right hand. Activity in second half concentrates on left hand with extended scales, alone and in various intervals with the right hand.

34 C Major
Tempestuous left-hand study opening with stepwise progression of a finger-crossing pattern that accompanies pompous dotted right-hand chords. Part 2 (mm. 17-31) opening with integration of a sustained tenor melody into the left-hand accompaniment pattern. Part 3 (mm. 32-43) dropping to a gently lyrical whisper before returning to a grandiose character.

35 A Major
Right-hand broken octaves in stepwise patterns. Second section featuring thirds alternating with arpeggiated crossovers (mm. 16-23).

36 C Major
Contrary motion study in diatonic/chromatic scales and arpeggios.

37 A♭ Major
Right-hand division into soprano melody and alto tremolos against left-hand octave stride bass. Broken ascending chromatic thirds in part 2 (mm. 16-22).

38 G Major
Right-hand trill/tremolo study in parallel thirds and sixths with interlocking and alternating left-hand parts.

39 D♭ Major
39 Right-hand arpeggios, primarily on black keys. A second section (mm. 25-48) moving through keys of G♭ Major, A♭ Minor, and C♭ Major.

40 F Major
Grand finale of the set with much variety and brilliance. Opening with right-hand 3-2-1 patterns with brief octave extensions (mm. 1-24), followed by section with measured trills and tremolos against detached opposite hand (mm. 25-49). Reciprocal alternating accompaniment introduced in m. 72.

ABOUT THE EDITOR

ary Busch is widely known to teaching organizations in the U.S., Canada, and Germany as performer, lecturer, adjudicator, and presenter of master classes. He received his performance training at the University of Washington under Béla Siki, Randolph Hokanson, and John Moore, and at the Manhattan School of Music with Artur Balsam. Dr. Busch is Professor of Music on the Piano and Music History faculties at the Crane School of Music, State University of New York at Potsdam, where he has been in residence since 1983. He has served on the board of directors of the New York Federation of Music Clubs, on the executive board of the New York State Music Teachers Association, and as Chair of Music Theory, History, and Composition at the Crane School of Music. Special areas of historical research and teaching include music of the Classic and Romantic periods, the art song, and the history of American music.

Notes

1 Carl Philipp Emanuel Bach's *Essay on the True Art of Playing Keyboard Instruments* (1753) constitutes one of the most important records of correct 18th-century keyboard style, including technique, thoroughbass, and improvisation. Haydn, Mozart, and Beethoven all studied earnestly from it.

2 Carl Czerny, "Recollections from My Life," trans. Ernest Sanders, *The Musical Quarterly*, XLII, No. 3 (July, 1956), 303.

3 Ibid., 307.

4 The style of Johann Nepomuk Hummel (1778-1837) represents the high point of Viennese pianism, a blend between Clementi's technique and that of Mozart, with whom he studied. Considered by many of his contemporaries to be the rival of Beethoven, Hummel's playing was virtuosic, elegant, and clean, although superficial.

5 Thoroughbass, or figured bass, was a system of indicating an accompaniment by bass notes marked with figures indicating intervals placed above the bass. It was used primarily throughout the Baroque period.

6 Carl Czerny, "Recollections from My Life," 314-15.

7 Ibid., 315.

8 Harold C. Schonberg, *The Great Pianists from Mozart to the Present* (New York: Fireside Books, 1963), 93.

9 K. Dale, "The Three C's: Pioneers of Pianoforte Playing," *Musical Review*, vi (1945), 138.

10 Ernst Hutcheson, *The Literature of the Piano*, revised and updated by Rudolph Ganz (New York: Alfred A. Knopf, 1964), 148.

11 Carl Czerny, *Complete Theoretical and Practical Pianoforte School*, Op. 500 (London: R. Cocks & Co., 1839), III, 100.

12 Reginald R. Gerig, *Famous Pianists and Their Technique* (Washington: Robert B. Luce, Inc., 1974), 229-30.

13 Sigismund Lebert (1822-1884) and Ludwig Stark (1831-1884), who in 1856 published the *Grosse Klavierschule* (*Grand Theoretical and Practical Piano School for Systematic Instruction in all Branches of Piano Playing from the First Elements to the Highest Perfection*), were the co-founders of the Royal Conservatory at Stuttgart.

14 Carl Czerny, *Complete Theoretical and Practical Pianoforte School*, I, 216-17.

15 Carl Czerny, *Letters to a Young Lady on the Art of Playing the Pianoforte* (New York: Hewitt & Jacques, 1837-1841), 6.

16 Carl Czerny, *Complete Theoretical and Practical Pianoforte School*, III, 15.

17 Ibid., 26.

18 Carl Czerny, *Letters to a Young Lady on the Art of Playing the Pianoforte*, 31-2.

19 Carl Czerny, *Complete Theoretical and Practical Pianoforte School*, III, 100.

BIBLIOGRAPHY

Czerny, Carl. *Complete Theoretical and Practical Pianoforte School*, Op. 500. London: R. Cocks & Co., 1839.

Czerny, Carl. *Letters to a Young Lady on the Art of Playing the Pianoforte*. New York: Hewitt & Jacques, 1837-41.

Czerny, Carl. "Recollections from My Life." Translated by Ernest Sanders. *The Musical Quarterly*, XLII, No. 3 (July 1956).

Dale, K. "The Three C's: Pioneers of Pianoforte Playing." *Musical Review*, vi (1945).

Gerig, Reginald R. *Famous Pianists and Their Technique*. Washington: Robert B. Luce, Inc., 1974.

Hutcheson, Ernst. *The Literature of the Piano*, revised and updated by Rudolph Ganz. New York: Alfred A. Knopf, 1964.

Schonberg, Harold C. *The Great Pianists from Mozart to the Present*. New York: Fireside Books, 1963.

DIE SCHULE DER GELÄUFIGKEIT

THE SCHOOL OF VELOCITY

Carl Czerny in 1839
Lithograph by S. Parmenter

The School of Velocity
Book One

Edited by Gary Busch

Carl Czerny

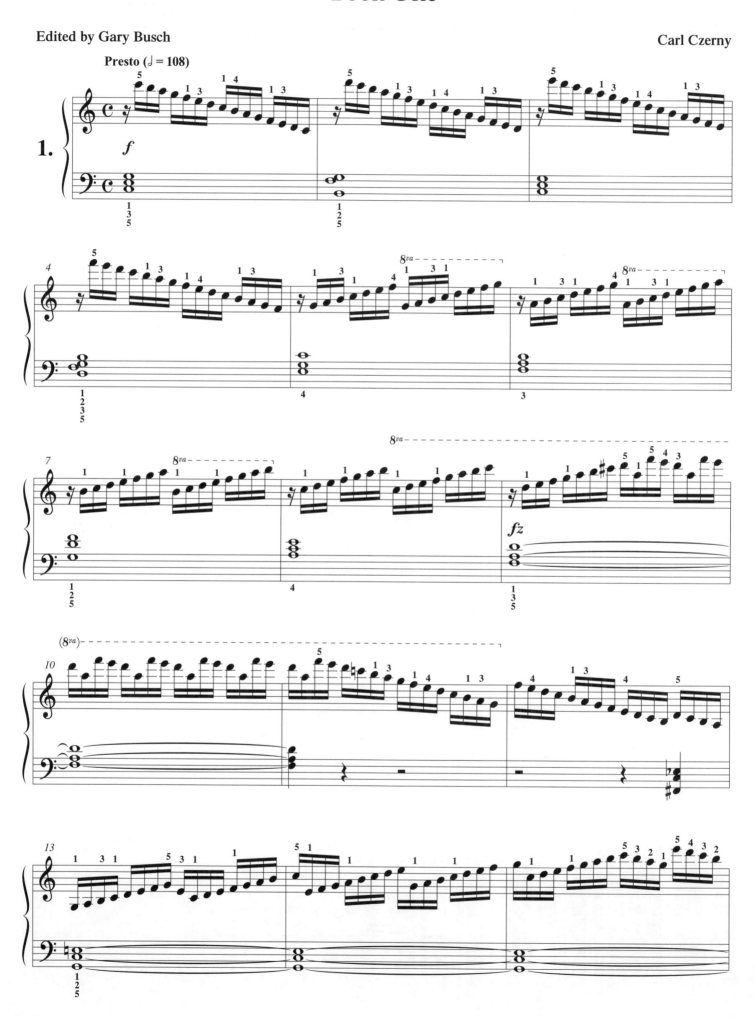

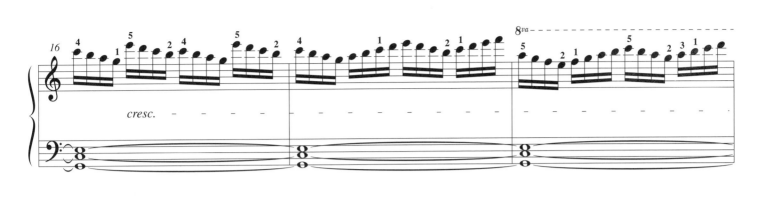

2. Molto allegro (♩ = 104)

6

Molto allegro (♩ = 108)

5.

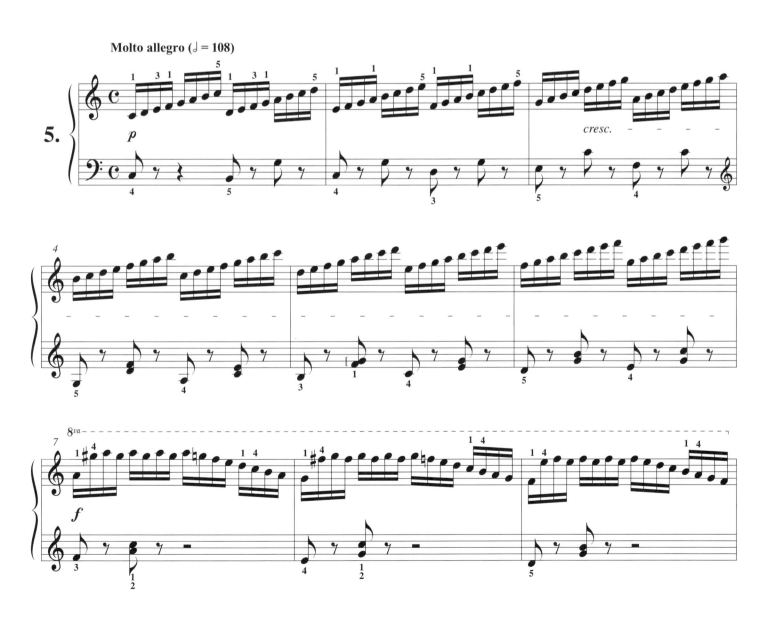

8

12

H1015

13

H1015

14

18

The School of Velocity
Book Two

11.

Molto allegro (♩ = 92)

12.

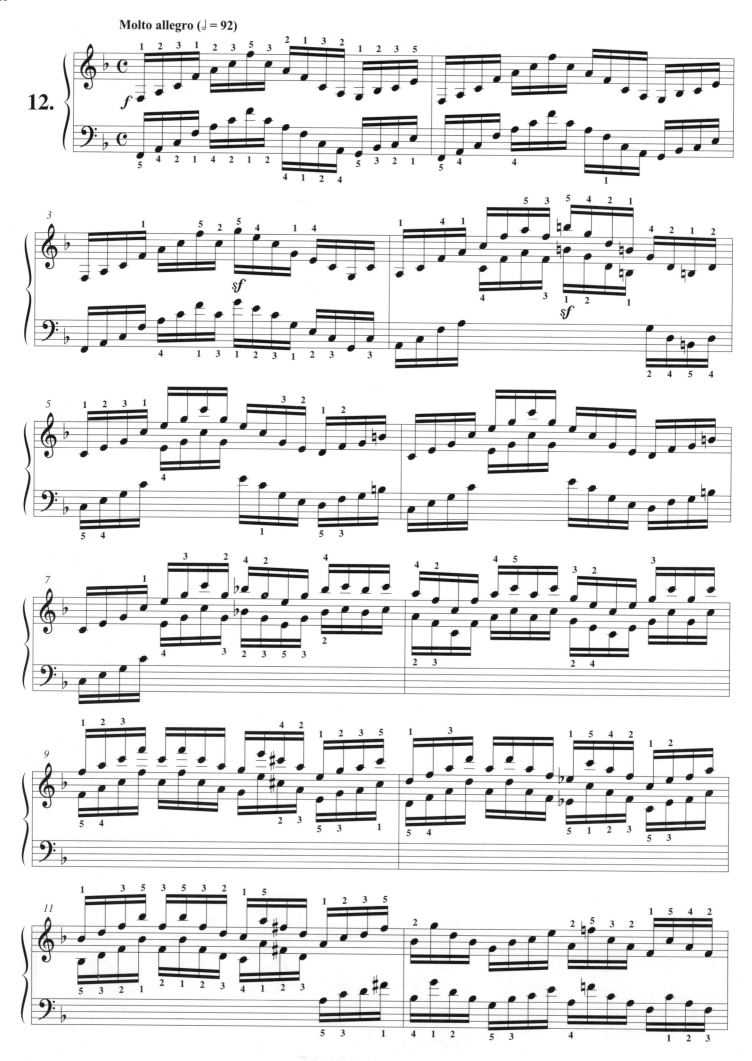

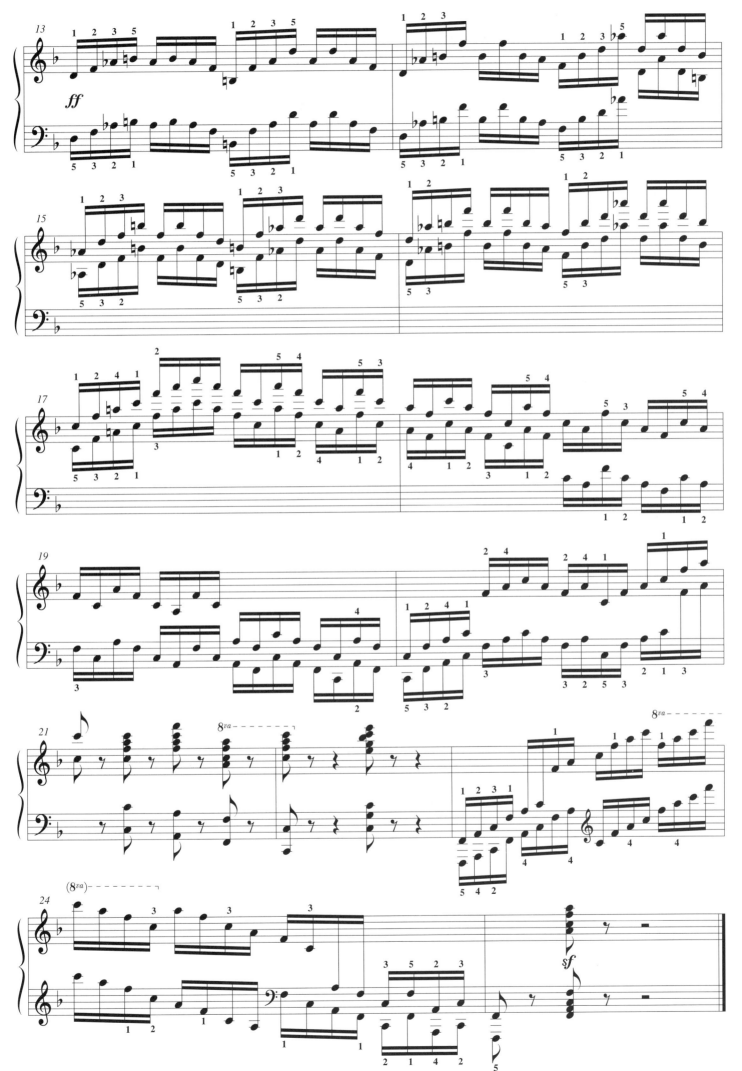

memory w/ no mistakes

Molto vivo e velocissimo (♩ = 116)

14.

Molto allegro (♩ = 96)

17.

42

44

19.

46

The School of Velocity
Book Three

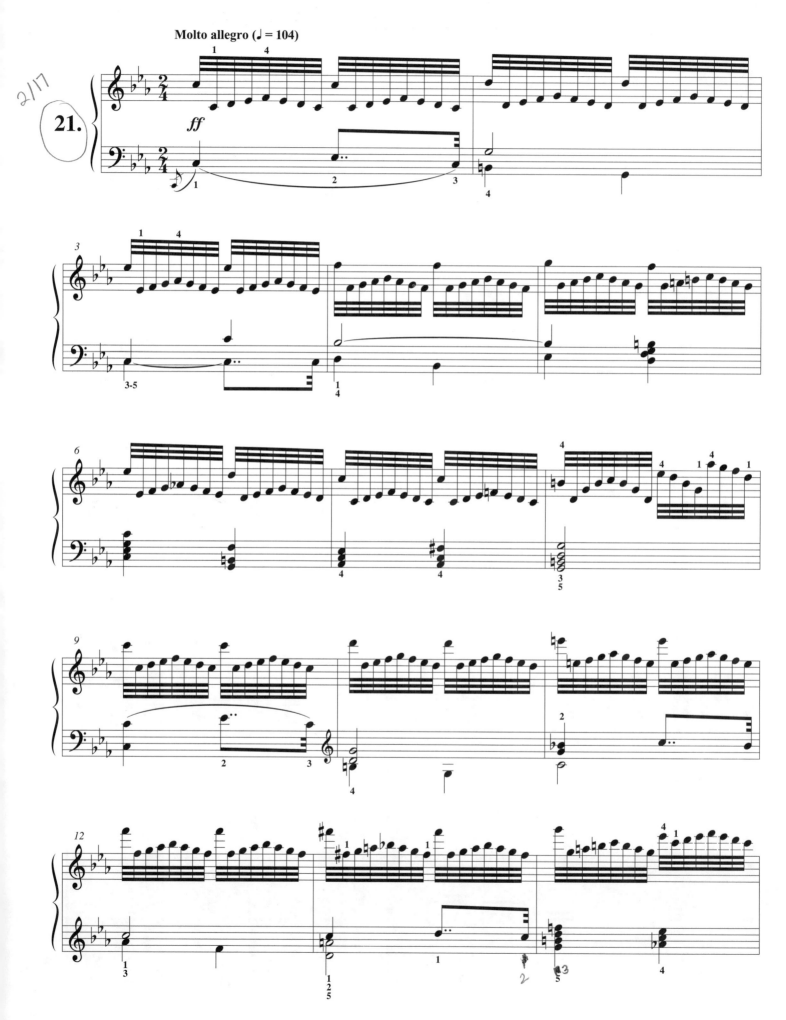

Molto allegro (♩ = 104)

21.

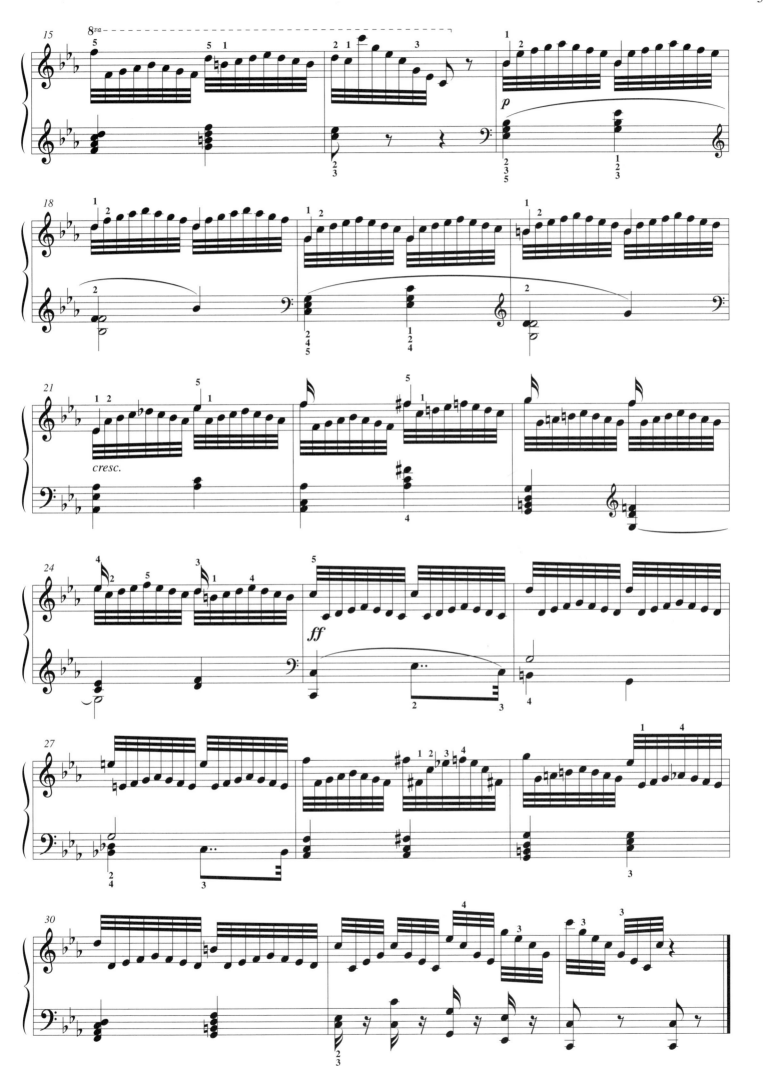

52

56

H1015

58

Molto allegro (♩ = 96)

25.

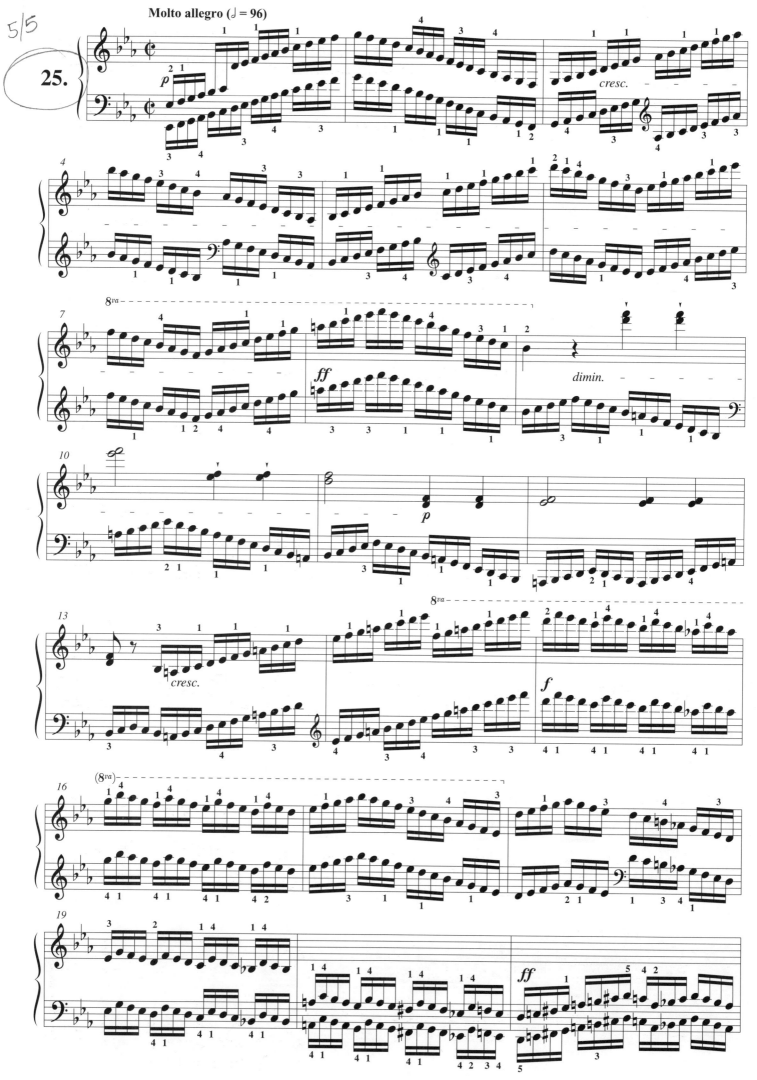

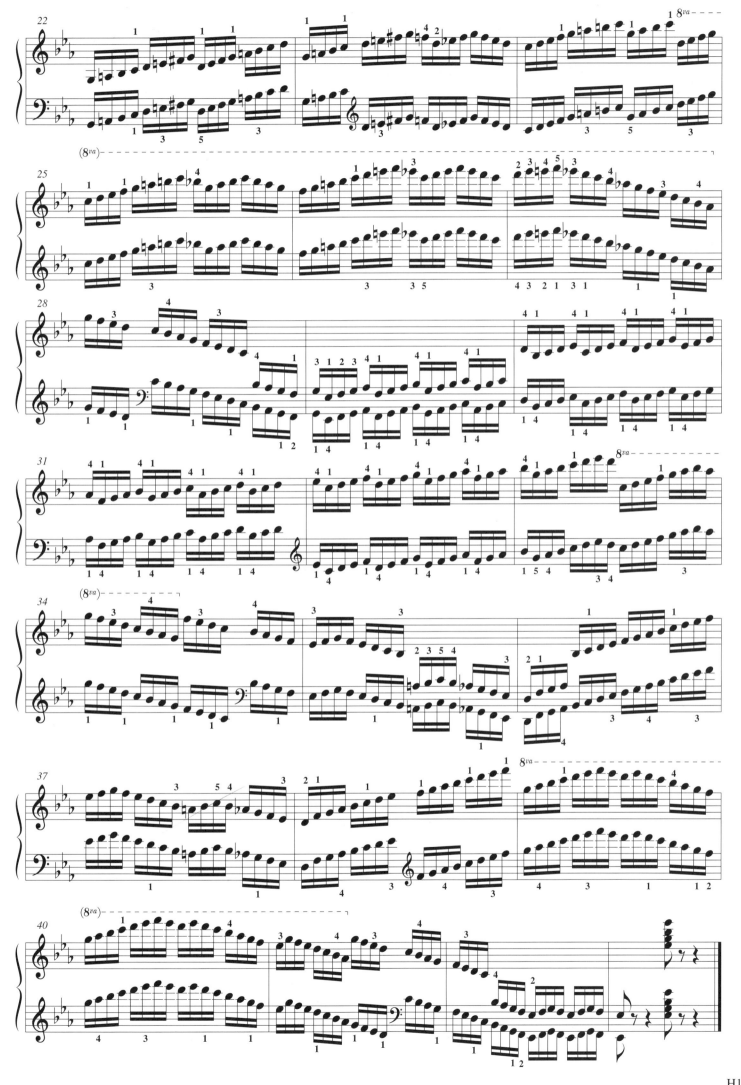

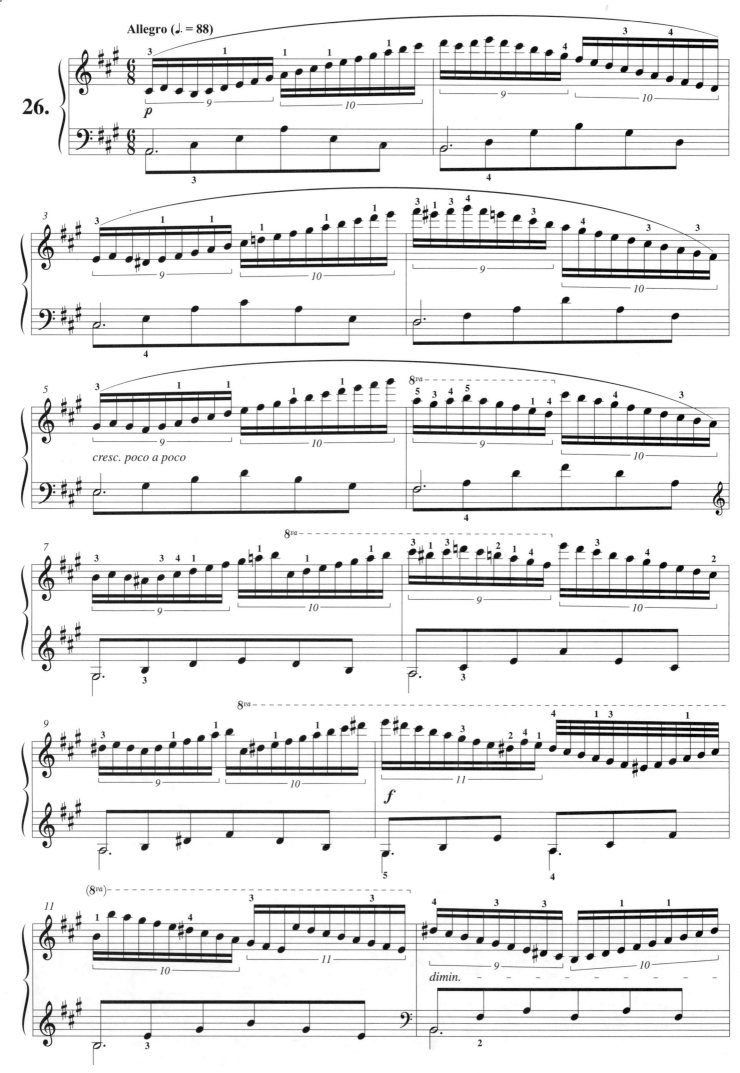

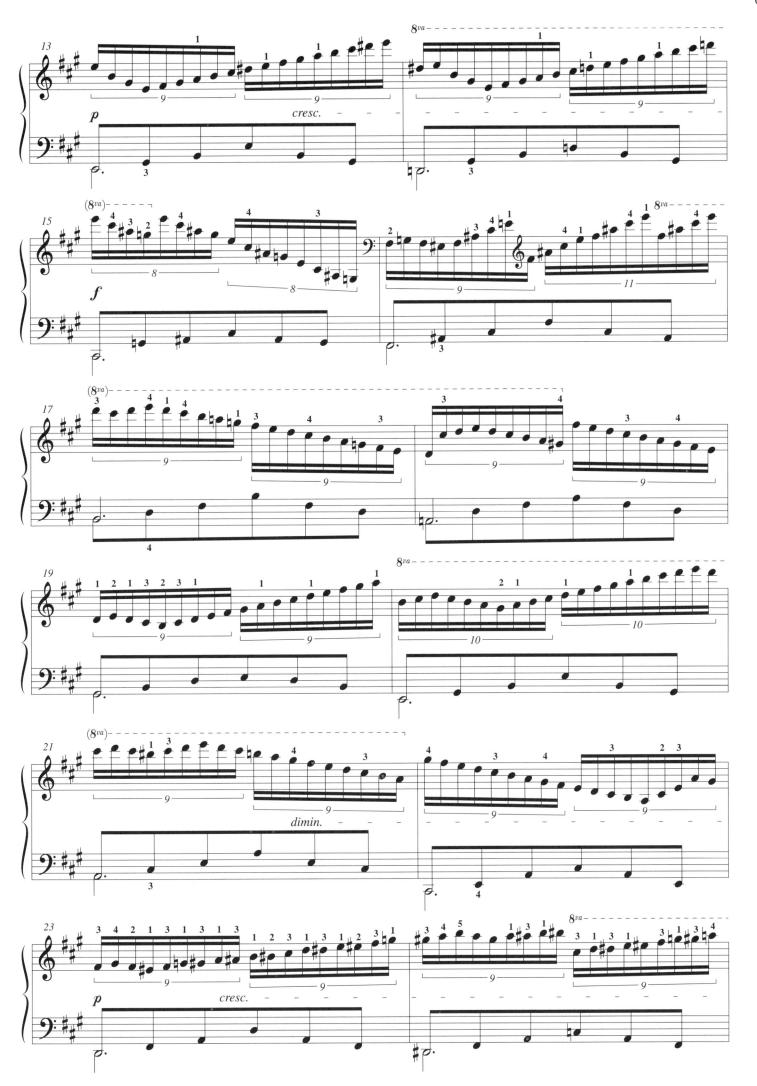

64

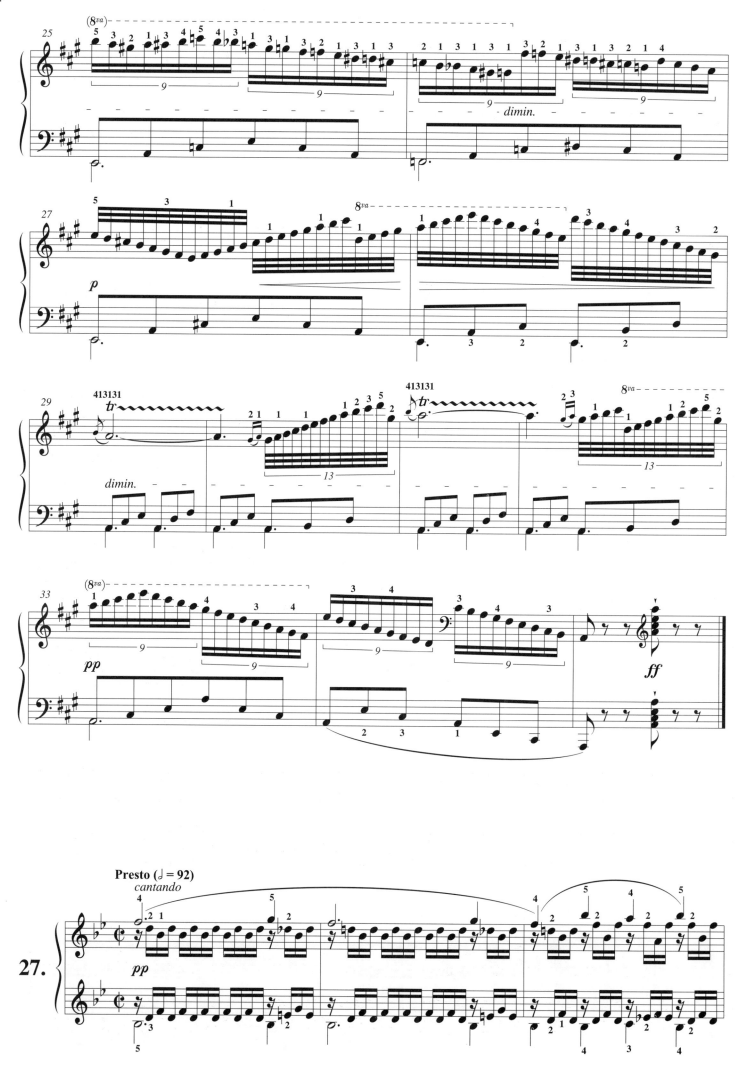

H1015

66

H1015

68

The School of Velocity
Book Four

Molto allegro (♩ = 60)

31.

74

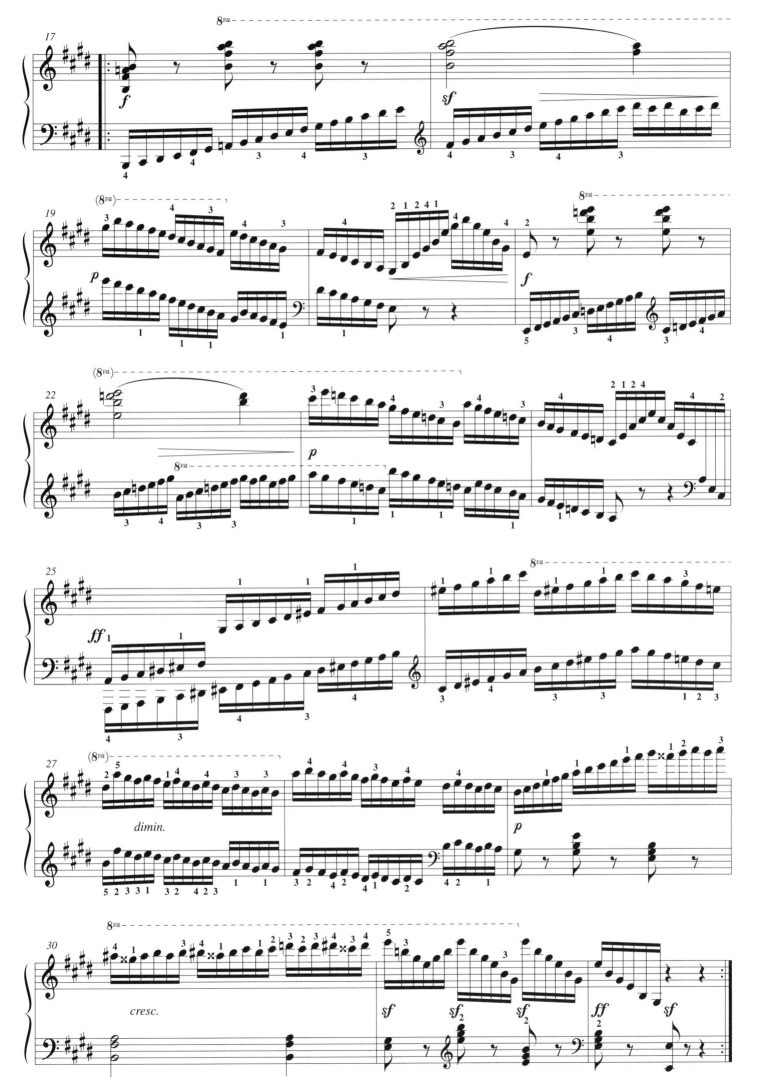

Allegro molto vivo ed energico (♩ = 88)

34.

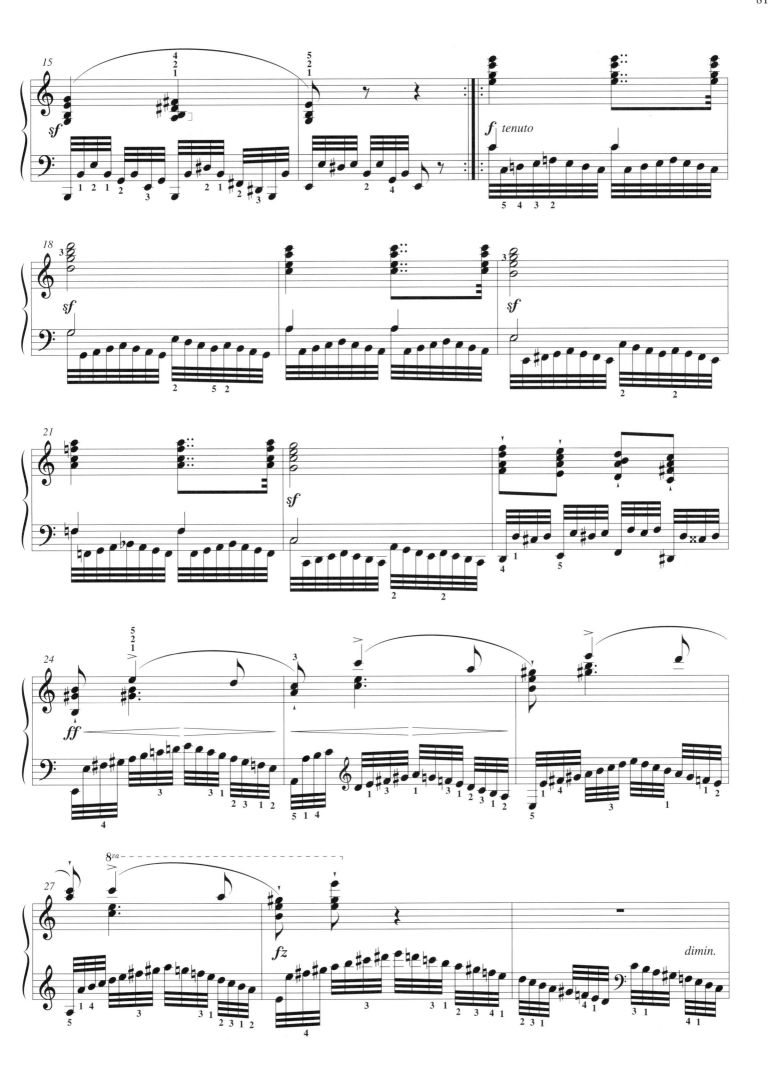

88

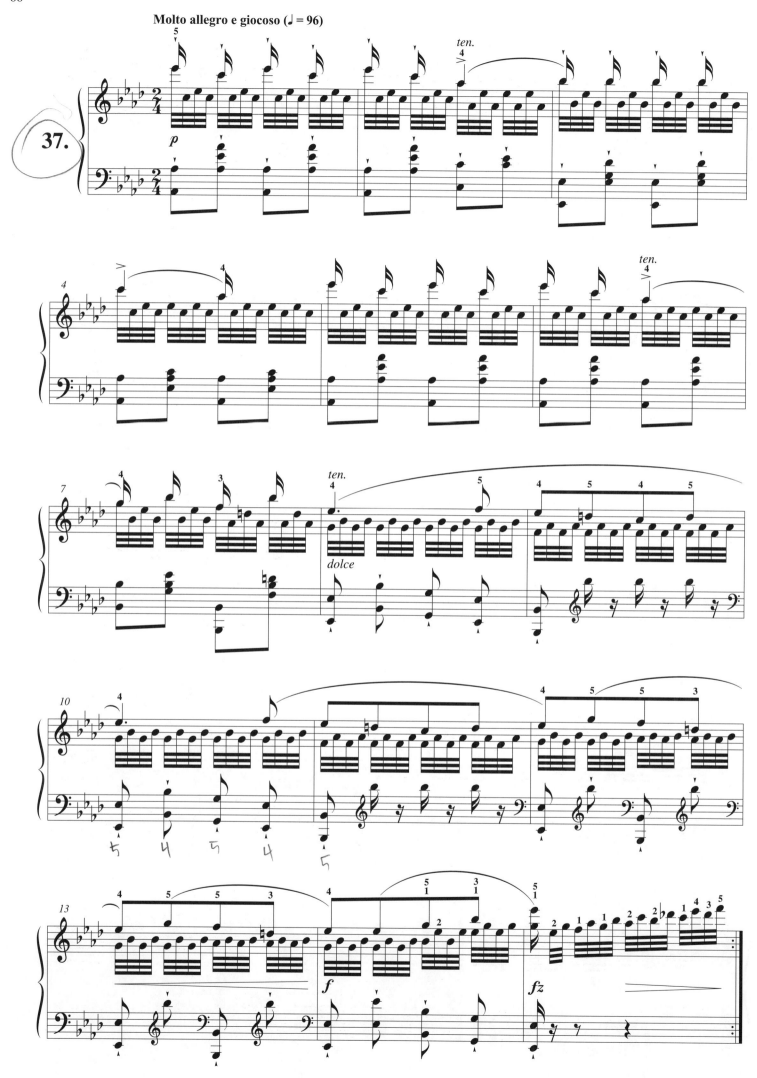

H1015

90

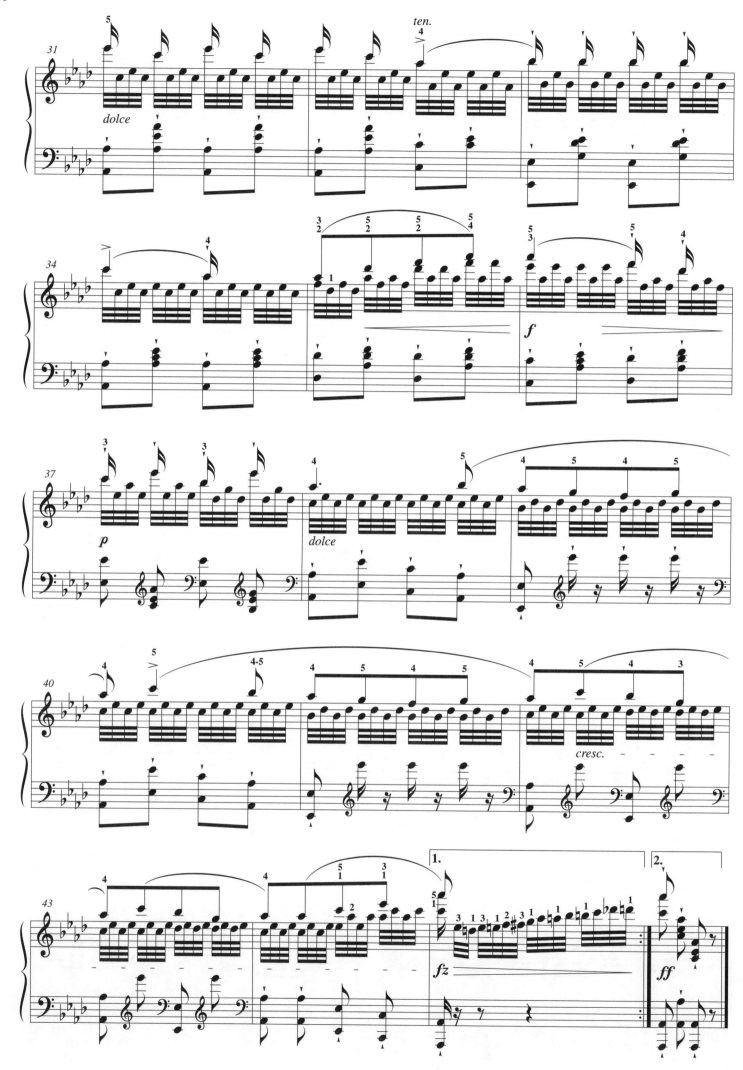

H1015

Molto allegro, quasi presto (♩ = 84)

92

H1015

94

Presto (à la Galopade) (♩ = 104)

39.

p leggiero

98

H1015

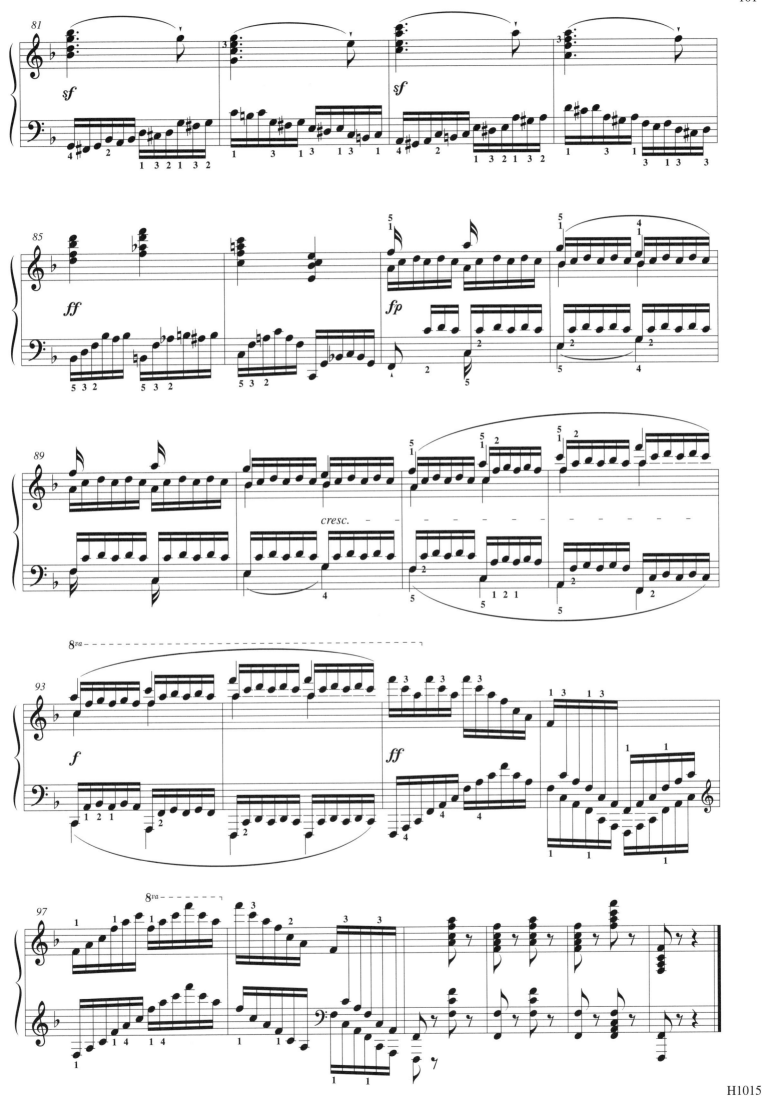